CALMING SKILLS WORKBOOK FOR KIDS 9-12

35+ Activities to Help Your Children Control their Behaviour, Master Emotions, Stop Losing their Temper, and Get Rid of their Frustration

By

Adrienne E.

The Star Publications

© **Copyright 2023 by The Star Publications - All rights reserved.**

Without the prior written permission of the Publisher, no part of this publication may be stored in a retrieval system, replicated, or transferred in any form or medium, digital, scanning, recording, printing, mechanical, or otherwise, except as permitted under 1976 United States Copyright Act, section 107 or 108. Permission concerns should be directed to the publisher's permission department.

Legal Notice

This book is copyright protected. It is only to be used for personal purposes. Without the author's or publisher's permission, you cannot paraphrase, quote, copy, distribute, sell, or change any part of the information in this book.

Disclaimer Notice

This book is written and published independently. Please keep in mind that the material in this publication is solely for educational and entertaining purposes. All efforts have provided authentic, up-to-date, trustworthy, and comprehensive information. There are no express or implied assurances. The purpose of this book's material is to assist readers in having a better understanding of the subject matter. The activities, information, and exercises are provided solely for self-help information. This book is not intended to replace expert psychologists, legal, financial, or other guidance. If you require counseling, please get in touch with a qualified professional.

By reading this text, the reader accepts that the author will not be held liable for any damages, indirectly or directly, experienced due to the use of the information included herein, particularly, but not limited to, omissions, errors, or inaccuracies. As a reader, you are accountable for your decisions, actions, and consequences.

ABOUT THE AUTHOR

Adrienne E. is a mindfulness mentor. She has written many books in her 10+ years of experience. Her favourite topics are positive parenting, raising happy and calm kids, and teaching mindfulness techniques to raise good children. She assists mothers in fostering greater harmony and collaboration within their households, and she helps the parents inspire and improve their kids' lives by developing good manners and coping skills. She has two energetic girls who push her every day to improve her skills and inspire the lives of others too.

CONTENTS

ABOUT THE AUTHOR	3
INTRODUCTION	7
MY BLUE DAYS	9
A MINDFUL APPROACH FOR PARENTS	10
CHAPTER 1: A GOOD BEHAVIOR WINS HEARTS	11
1.1 Reasons for Bad Behavior in Kids	11
1.2 Differentiating Good and Bad Behaviors in Daily Life	13
Bad Behaviors	13
Good Behaviors	14
1.3 When Your Worries Get Too Big, Deal with them Mindfully	15
1.4 Good Behavior Turns Your kid into a Leader	23
Indoor Activities	23

CHAPTER 2: MASTER EMOTIONS AND STOP LOSING TEMPER — 27

2.1 Fighting and Bullying Makes Your Kid Anxious — 27

2.2 Let Your Kids Be the Masters of Their Emotions — 32

2.3 Importance of Outdoor Activities to Master Emotions — 35

The Story of a Grumpy Monkey — 38

CHAPTER 3: MASTERING FRUSTRATION: HELP YOUR KIDS NOT TO BECOME A GRUMPY MONKEY — 40

3.1 Frustration and Loss of Focus — 40

3.2 What Makes Your Kid Frustrated? — 41

3.3 Help Your Kids Stay Calm — 43

Indoor Calming Activities — 43

Outdoor Activities — 45

3.4 Why Not Help Kids to be Cool Like a Cucumber? — 45

Different Breathing Techniques — 47

CHAPTER 4: HELP YOUR KID FIND CALMNESS THROUGH CBT 52

4.1 Effectiveness and Importance of CBT for Kids 52

Effectiveness of CBT 53

Importance of CBT 54

4.2 Helping Kids Cope with Stress, Anxiety, and Anger Through CBT 55

4.3 Want Your Kids to Have More Control Over Their Temper through CBT? 63

WHAT DID YOU LEARN? 73

FINAL WORDS 74

GOODBYE MESSAGE FOR KIDS! 75

INTRODUCTION

Do you get screamed at when you stop your kids from doing something they want to do?

How often does your kid apologize to you after screaming and getting mad at you?

Do you want your kids to control their emotions and learn to calm themselves before anything bad happens?

Well, I am here to help you if you want your kids to get rid of their frustration without trying too hard. First, you need to understand that irrational behavior when kids are angry and sad does not make them bad kids. This behavior is not appreciated, however, it can be easily fixed by teaching your kids how to control it with understanding and effort.

How does this book help one to master their emotions? The answer is very simple. Being a behavioral therapist, I know many kids with the same problem, and my own son used to act out whenever I asked him to do something he did not want to do. I helped him control his emotions and calm down that avoided anything bad from happening.

In the first chapter of the book, you will learn about the differences between accepted or good behaviors and unaccepted or bad behaviors in kids. You will also learn about the things that can make your kids angry and lose control over their emotions and how to teach your kids to control them. The first chapter also includes various mindful activities to help kids deal with their emotions. You will also learn about the importance of emotional control and how good behavior can help your kids to become good leaders.

The second chapter of the book is all about learning good manners and how can kids ask for the things they want calmly. You will also learn why cursing and getting angry is bad and how to stop kids from doing it. The second chapter will help your kids master their emotions using outdoor activities and learn about the importance of a healthy body and a healthy mind.

Chapter three of the book is specific to the kids who are angry most of the time and it discusses how can we help such kids become calmer and more focused. When you are a grumpy monkey, you lose focus and interest, and become frustrated. Chapter three will also help you find out the reasons for your kids' frustration and give you a plethora of the activities that will help you teach your kids how to better control their emotions.

In the fourth chapter of the book, you will find various Cognitive Behavioral Therapy (CBT) exercises and activities and learn how to effectively use these techniques to help your kids cope up with anger, stress, and other strong negative emotions. This section is specifically designed to help create a bond between parents and kids, and the activities in this chapter are to be done by kids in the presence of their parents.

If you are enjoying the book, why not read it till the end and teach your kids emotional control and regulation?

MY BLUE DAYS

Let me tell you the story of a kid who used to slam doors and drag his feet along the floor without any reason. Do you know what he used to do? Well, when his parents did not let him play video games for too many hours, he would get angry and slam the door. He would shout at them and tell them how much he hated them. After a few hours, he would come crying to his parents for acting out and say how sorry he was, "I am sorry, I did not mean to do that."

Does this situation sound familiar to you? How often have you done the same? How often have you shouted at your parents for not buying you a toy you really wanted? How many times did you feel bad about not playing video games? You always apologized later, but what if you could control yourself and calm down before things escalated?

It is normal to feel angry and sad. Everyone has blue days once in a while. You can always realize when you have acted unacceptably, but how to control it before any damage happens is the question. Through this book, I will help you answer this because I have dealt with many kids with the same problem, and eventually they all learned to calm themselves when needed.

I understand your need to shout when you are angry and you do not get your way with things. It is natural. Humans can have more than 10,000 thoughts daily, and we cannot control every thought. This is why it is important to learn self-control through various activities to understand which thoughts to act on and which ones to let go of.

This book will help you in calming yourself when you are angry through several fun activities for you. Let's start with the hope that by the end of this book, you will have learned some calming skills and mastered your emotions.

A MINDFUL APPROACH FOR PARENTS

Are you worried about your kid acting out every time they do not get their favorite toy or extra play time? Do you see them stomping their feet or throwing stuff around when they are mad at you? Are you looking to understand why and how to teach your kid how to calm down when needed? If you answered yes to any of these questions, welcome to my world, where I dealt with the same situation when my kid was ten.

I always heard my son stomping his feet whenever I took the controller of his PS4, even after hours of gameplay! He would later apologize to me, but he always acted out in these situations. This is one of the main reasons I had to understand the reasons and causes of kids' irrational behavior.

Do you know that skills development starts at the age of 3? Kids between the ages of 9-12 have hundreds of thousands of thoughts throughout the day, and their brains are not developed enough to help them understand which thoughts to act on and which ones to let go of. We can help them learn self-regulation and master their emotions through various activities in this book that will help your kids to calm down when they are angry or frustrated.

Let's begin the book with the hope that by the end, your kid will be better at controlling their emotions!

We have included a section of questions at the end to record the progress you have made through this book. Let's begin!

CHAPTER 1: A GOOD BEHAVIOR WINS HEARTS

Everyone always talks about how bad behavior is unacceptable and how it affects daily life, personal relationships, and friendships, but no one ever talks about how a good behavior helps in winning hearts. There are several reasons kids can have irrational outbursts. Let's learn about the most common reasons for kids to lose their emotional control and how they can get better at controlling their emotions and using their good behavior to succeed in life.

1.1 REASONS FOR BAD BEHAVIOR IN KIDS

Kids from ages 9-12 grow rapidly, and their senses are heightened due to the level of energy they have. They cannot tell you what they are feeling as they are less expressive with words, but their actions can tell you everything about their emotions. Parents with kids in this age group are often worried about their kids' behavior whose actions can be questionable and unacceptable most of the time. This can be due to several reasons including trouble at school, playgrounds, or even home.

Identifying the problem and its cause is the first step to finding the solution. So, let's learn some of the most common reasons for kids' bad behavior and try to find the solution for each of these.

ANXIETY

The most common reason for kids' outbursts and strong, uncontrolled emotions is anxiety, and it not only makes kids shy and timid but can also make them angry and stubborn.

Most kids cannot handle pressure and expectations well because of being in the development phase of their lives where they are learning new things every day, and when they feel anxious about any situation, they start to show anger and discomfort by lashing out at others. Anxiety can lead to disruptive behavior, and parents must be on the lookout for their kids' anxiety and its triggers.

For example, if your kid has social anxiety, try to avoid criticizing them in public because it will put more pressure on them and trigger their anxiety which will lead to disruptive behavior.

LACK OF ATTENTION AND CARE

Kids need constant attention and care, and when they feel left out, they tend to throw tantrums to get attention. If your kid shows anger by fighting with their siblings or throwing and breaking stuff frequently, you must increase your attention and care for them.

IMITATION

If your kid is acting out regularly, there is a chance that either you or someone they know is behaving in the same manner when they are frustrated. Kids learn to behave from what they see in their parents, teachers, or anyone around them, and can also imitate the behaviors of a characters from TV shows or cartoons.

Therefore, you need to be careful about your behavior in front of your kids and keep in touch with their school to see if any of the other kids or teachers behave irrationally when they are frustrated. Also, you need to monitor the exposure of your kid to violent and unaccepted behavior shown in games or cartoons. As a parent, you should step up and be a role model to your kids by showing them good behavior.

RESTLESSNESS

Restlessness is another common reason for kids with anger issues. When kids are restless because of being unwell, hungry, or tired, they become moody, often resulting in tantrums and frustration.

If your kid has a habit of throwing stuff routinely and getting frustrated and angry, you need to make sure to be more careful about their health and well-being. Sometimes the tantrums could be a signal toward a prolonged illness. Make sure your kids are not restless, hungry, or ill.

AUTISM AND ADHD

Kids with autism and ADHD are more often involved in behaviors that are inappropriate and unaccepted. Bad behaviors are in no way specific for kids with ADHD and autism, however, they are most likely to behave irrationally, frustrated, and angry as compared to kids without ADHD.

SOLUTION

Parents should spend more time with their kids and ask them about their daily interactions and routine. There is a strong chance that most of the problems related to behavior will be solved just through communication. If not, there are numerous activities and worksheets in this book for kids that will surely help them with learning calming skills.

1.2 DIFFERENTIATING GOOD AND BAD BEHAVIORS IN DAILY LIFE

Sometimes kids are unaware of good manners and behaviors, and continue to behave in an irrational and unaccepted manner until they are told otherwise. Let's look at some of these behaviors and help our kids learn the difference between good and bad behavior.

BAD BEHAVIORS

DISRESPECT

Throwing tantrums and getting angry is normal for kids between the ages of 9-12, however, there is a difference between getting frustrated and being disrespectful. Parents should look out for disrespectful behaviors such as talking back to adults and let their kids know the difference between a difference of opinion and disrespect.

The best solution to this problem is to communicate with kids, talk to them, give them a light penalty such as canceling their playtime until they learn their mistake and try to be more respectful, and give a reward for good behavior to recognize and encourage it.

BULLYING

Bullying is one of the main reasons kids show anger and frustration. If your kid is being bullied and cannot do anything about it, they may get frustrated and release their anger on others. Most school-going kids face this problem to some extent, but what if your kid is actually the bully, and throwing things around and being disrespectful is their way to bully others? Always keep a close eye on your kids' behavior and find out the reasons for their extra-aggressive behavior. If you sense any disrespect or teasing in their behavior, make sure they understand bullying is harmful and unacceptable.

LYING AND CHEATING

Lying and cheating are mostly ignored in young kids, but they should not be. Imaginative play and thinking creatively to get out of a situation are often considered good, but when kids become habitual in lying, make sure to show them why lying and cheating are bad. Never appreciate kids' cheating on a board game and encourage them to fair play.

GOOD BEHAVIORS

HELPING OTHERS

Helping others and taking care of others' needs should be encouraged in kids to introduce them to good behaviors. It will help them understand others and give them the respect they deserve.

PRAISING

Kids should be encouraged to praise others when they see something good. It develops their communication skills and encourages good behavior.

ACTIVITY FOR GOOD AND BAD BEHAVIORS

Making kids understand the difference between good and bad behaviors is the first step toward encouraging good behavior. No one can force kids to stop throwing things around when they are frustrated until they understand that tantrums and talking back are unacceptable behaviors.

The activity below involves both the parents and the kids and requires them to note down every good and bad thing they did the whole week to familiarize kids with good and bad behaviors.

- Take a piece of paper and mark each day on it.

- Write down the display of good or bad behavior for each day in front of that day.

- If at the end of the week, the score of good behavior is more than bad behavior, reward your kid by giving them an extra hour of gameplay.

- For the opposite, try spending time with you kids to explain to them why it is more important to have a good behavior.

This activity will help and encourage kids to behave well throughout the week while trying to improve each week.

1.3 WHEN YOUR WORRIES GET TOO BIG, DEAL WITH THEM MINDFULLY

Kids are often unaware of their emotions and need someone to explain to them their feelings. You can help your kid understand their emotions with the activities given below. Kids can complete the following activities daily to further understand their emotions and build good habits.

UNDERSTANDING EMOTIONS

This activity will help your kid understand their emotions. Ask them to color their emotions according to how they feel that day. For example, they can color the anger part if they feel angry and the sad part of the wheel if they feel sad.

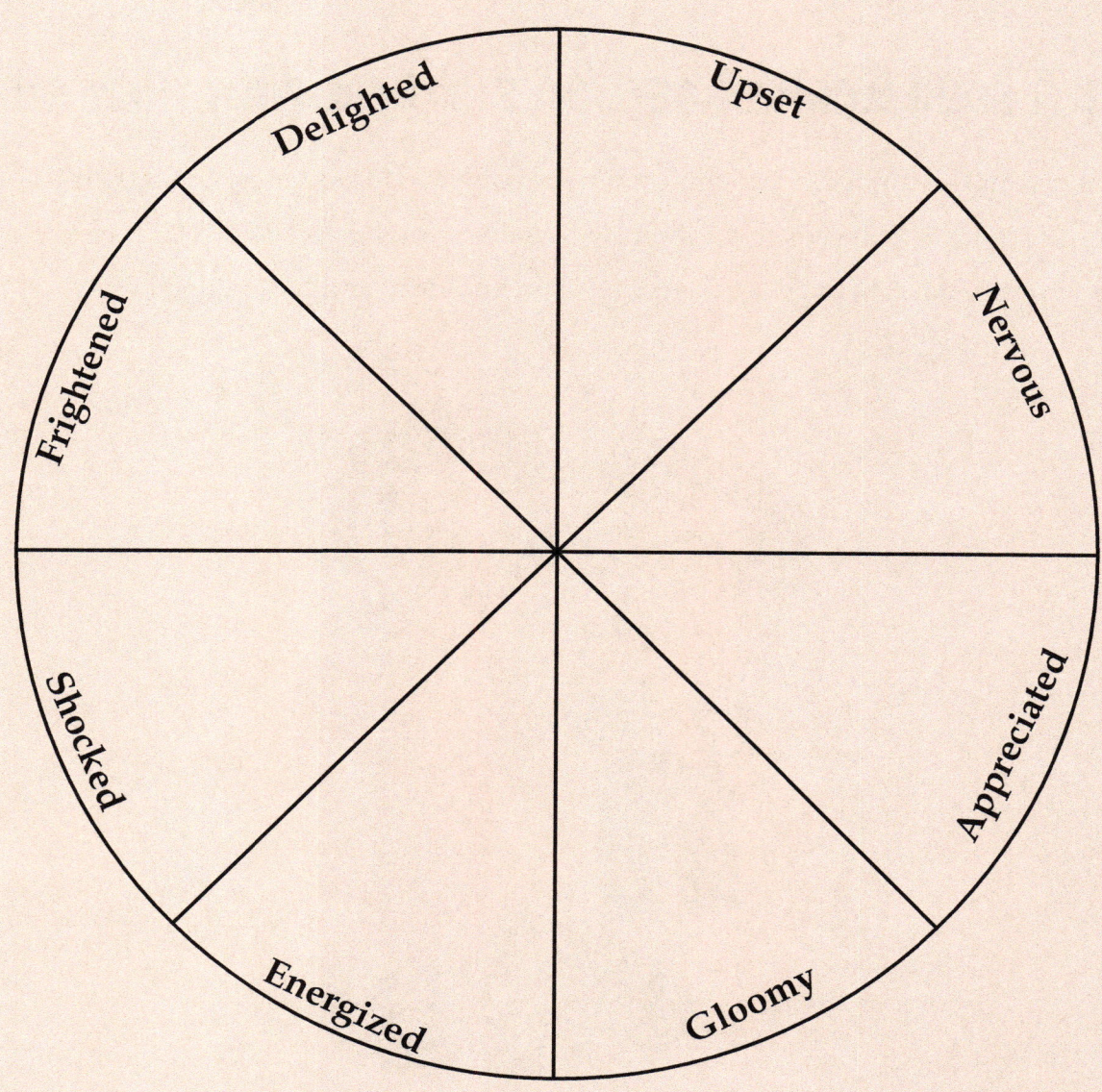

MINDFUL ACTIVITIES

Solve the following riddles with your kids when they feel frustrated and angry. This section is for parents and kids to perform together. Take turns, one by one and ask each other different riddles so the kids can calm themselves down and get rid of their frustration.

What is that one thing that can be served but not be eaten? **A TENNIS BALL**	What is that one thing that can be caught, but not thrown? **A COLD**
Where can you quickly enter but struggle to exit? **TROUBLE**	Which sort of band does not play songs? **A RUBBER BAND**
Mother of Ryan has three kids. The name of the first kid is SNAP. The name of the second kid is Crackle. What is the name of the third child? **RYAN**	When it comes to height, what might leap farther than just a framework? _____

What are the two foods that a person could not eat in breakfast?

LUNCH AND DINNER

What is really black whenever its clean yet white whenever it's filthy?

A CHALKBOARD

What food item do you frequently stock up on but are unable to eat?

A PLATE

What is something which rises and falls without changing location?

THE TEMPERATURE

What is something that you have to crack in order to utilize it?

_____

What can you touch with your left hand that you can't with your right?

YOUR RIGHT ELBOW

What is it that you own, however your pals make more frequent use of it than you do?

YOUR NAME

What grows in size as amount is reduced?

A HOLE

Who or what consists only of a head and a tail?

A COIN

To what query can you never reply "yes"?

_____

GLITTER JAR

MY GLITTER BOTTLE FOR STRESS RELIEF

- Here, have a jar or plastic bottle ready for your kid to decorate.

- After filling the bottle with water at around 80% capacity, add transparent glue, food coloring, and glitter.

- Wrap the top in hot glue, give it a good shake, and enjoy watching the glitter fall to the bottom.

This activity will help your kid calm down by watching a calming glittery flow in the bottle. Let them have fun making the glitter flow!

HOW IS THE WEATHER?

Naming your emotions according to different weather types is helpful for kids in many ways. It gives them control over emotions and teaches them that just like the weathers come and go, emotions do too. Help your kid perform the activity given below to have more control over their emotions.

MY EMOTIONS CLOUD

WHAT'S THE WEATHER LIKE RIGHT NOW?

- Teach your kid that the weather has a direct correlation to how they're feeling (good mood when it's sunny, sadness when it's cloudy, and so on).
- Much like the weather, feelings change.
- It's natural to experience a wide range of feelings, and giving them names gives us control over them.

FEEL THE BEAT

This activity helps kids on multiple levels including calming their nerves down, helping them become more mindful, and improving their focus. Ask your kid to perform the following activities and feel their heartbeat at the end.

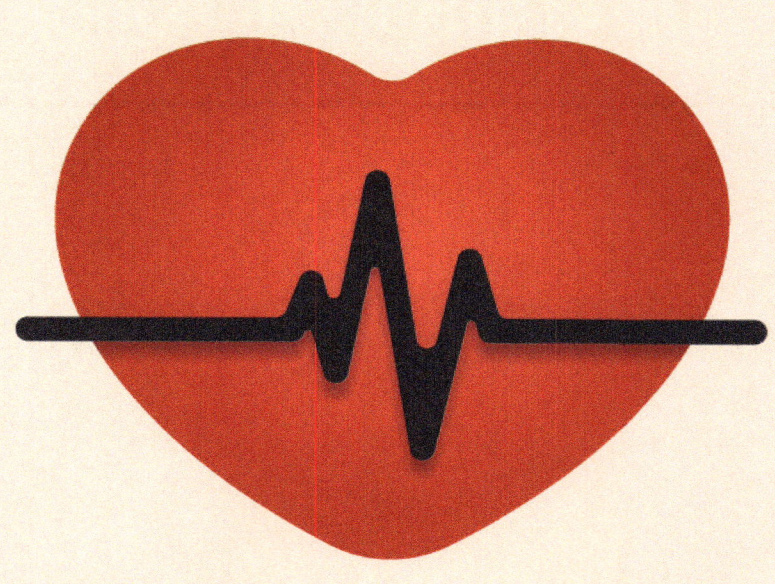

FOCUS ON YOUR HEARTBEAT

- **Put your kid through a minute of jumping jacks or up-and-down hopping.**
- **Then, have them take a seat and put a hand on their chest.**
- **Try to get them to focus on their heart rate and feel it beating.**

1.4 GOOD BEHAVIOR TURNS YOUR KID INTO A LEADER

Nothing can encourage kids to behave well unless they understand the importance of and the rewards a good behavior can bring. Use sports and other outdoor activities to encourage and instill calmness and emotional control in kids.

WHEN YOU TALK CALMLY, PEOPLE LISTEN

Kids need to understand that when they are polite and behave nicely, people will listen to them more and follow them. Parents can encourage this behavior in kids by rewarding them when they act calmly.

MAKE THEM LEADERS

Use sports and outdoor activities to help kids understand that when they are calm, they can be great leaders. Take them to a football game and show them how players respond to every action on the playing field based on how you talk to them.

Arrange a football game between your child and their friends. In the first half, ask them to be rude to one of their friends on purpose. When they shout angrily or be disrespectful to others, they will notice that none of their friends are listening to them, and it will discourage this kind of behavior.

In the second half, ask them to stay calm and talk politely to their friends. The good response they will get from their friends will surely show them the benefits of talking nicely to others and it will encourage them to stay calm, composed, and friendly to others.

INDOOR ACTIVITIES

SPORTS

Make two teams of three kids each and complete the following activity by asking the questions set out below or any other questions related to your favorite sport from each other.

LET'S TALK

Discourse about the most watched sporting event in the world.

Discuss the sport you enjoy the most.

Jogging, you say?

Elaborate on the fascination with sports that so many people have.

Chit-chat about the winter sports that you enjoy.

24

FOOD

Food is the best topic to discuss among kids. Make two groups and perform the activity below.

LET'S TALK

Share the recipe for your go-to meal and the story behind how you came to love it.

Discuss the worst things you've ever eaten.

Provide your reasons for the need of eating right.

Share your thoughts on the best eatery in your town and the reasons you go it so often.

Share stories about the traditional foods of your homeland.

QUESTIONNAIRE

Make two teams with five kids on each team. Answer all the questions in the image below on a piece of paper and read your answers loudly when all the players are done answering.

LET'S GET TO KNOW EACH OTHER!

SPORTS

Have you ever received a medal or trophy for your athletic accomplishments?
Has football been your most recent sport?
Are you a marathon runner?

TRAVELLING

Did you have any ocean swimming experience this year?
If so, where did you go?
Is summer travel already in the works for you?

DIFFICULTIES

Have you ever been in a vehicle or bike accident?
What about financial losses?
How often do your parents give you a time-out?

CLOTHES

Do your shoes need to be cleaned?
Do you ever wear pre-loved or vintage clothing?
When was the last time you went shopping for clothes?

ANIMALS

Have you visited the Zoo this year?
Do you have any dog-kissing experience?
Are you an experienced horseback rider?

CHAPTER 2: MASTER EMOTIONS AND STOP LOSING TEMPER

It is vital to help your kid control their anger to develop calmness in their personality. This chapter will discuss how to keep kids calm and composed and why it is important to control hate and anger.

This chapter is specially designed for kids who struggle with uncontrolled emotions and staying calm in different situations. Let's teach kids more about how to act and react in different situations.

2.1 FIGHTING AND BULLYING MAKES YOUR KID ANXIOUS

Facing a bully is one of the main reasons a kid can feel anxious. The first thing parents should do is to visit their school and playgrounds where they spend most of their time. Observe kids' behavior and interaction with everyone around them and watch their actions closely to find the connection between their frustration and behavior.

FIGHTING ANXIETY AND BULLYING

If you see your kid hesitant to go to a park or school, they might be getting bullied, causing them anxiety and ultimately affecting their control over emotions. The best way to deal with this situation is to talk to your kid, show an interest in their challenges and ask them to open up about their emotions. Opening up about emotions and how one is feeling helps in getting the emotions back in control.

LACK OF SELF-LOVE

One of the main reasons kids start to doubt themselves and feel anxious after a fight or being bullied is the sense of low self-esteem and self-love. Teach kids self-love and elevate their self-esteem through various techniques.

Complete the following activities to elevate self-esteem and help your kids love themselves and stand up against a bully.

NEGATIVE SELF-TALK MAY REALLY GET US DOWN!

Fill out each petal with a self-affirming thought.

IN THE HEARTS GIVEN BELOW, WRITE DOWN EVERYTHING THAT YOU LOVE ABOUT YOURSELF!

SOCIAL SKILLS

Learning basic social skills helps kids become less vulnerable to bullies and stay calm and composed when they are attacked by a bully.

COMMUNICATION SKILLS

If a kid has basic communication skills, they can fend off any bullying by using their words wisely and being more confident and firmer in their approach. Here are some things kids could say to the bullies more often;

"Do not bother me, this is my turn, and you will have to wait for your turn."

"Stop that! You are hurting me and it is not nice."

"You should ask before you touch me."

"I have a name, call me by my name, or do not call me at all."

Communication skills are not only important for kids to fight off bullies, but they are also important in learning at school. Teach your kids basic communication skills.

PATIENCE

Learning to be patient is the first step toward mastering emotions and calming skills. There are several times during the day when kids could feel frustrated, and the best way to deal with it is to teach them patience.

HOW TO TEACH KIDS TO BE PATIENT?

- Make schedules.
- Teach kids time management.
- Plan a trip and make all the preparations ahead of time, but cancel at the last minute. This activity will teach kids to be patient and cope with failed plans to get them ready for their adult lives.

Take them on the planned trip the next day as a reward for being patient and not throwing tantrums.

EMPATHY

Empathy is a basic social skill that every parent needs to teach their kid. It helps kids to consider the feelings of others and stay calm during times of discomfort and distress. When kids are empathic, they can master their emotions without much effort.

HOW TO TEACH KIDS TO BE EMPATHIC?

Empathy does not come overnight, and kids needs time to learn that. But, parents can help kids with empathy, for example, if kids are playing in a group and two kids want to play with the same thing, teach your kid to take turns and share instead of making one kid cry about it. Continuous practice of the same thing can teach your kid to be empathic and eventually respectful of others' feelings while also learning self-control and calming skills.

POSITIVITY

Teaching kids to stay positive will help them remain calm even in uncomfortable situations. This skill will eventually help kids with self-love and increase their self-esteem, which is an important part of the emotional regulation process.

With the benefits of positivity in mind, you should teach your child to be optimistic and to be able to change bad ideas into positive ones. There are several techniques for turning negative ideas into constructive ones:

- Crafting something using the raw materials at home, including matchsticks, glue, cotton, etc.
- Drawing something while trying to be creative with your imagination.
- Listening to music and dance.
- Taking a step back and thinking about why you are having a particular negative thought.

2.2 LET YOUR KIDS BE THE MASTERS OF THEIR EMOTIONS

Kids do need to master the art of living by learning different academic and social skills, however, emotional regulation is the one that keeps all the other skills intact since emotions can impact other skills such as problem-solving or creative thinking abilities.

The success of kids in this regard requires a healthy body and healthy mind; to be physically fit, mental health has to be at its 100%. Mastering the art of being in charge of emotions is not easy, especially for kids from ages 9-12. They have to learn a range of different academic concepts and skills, which can shift their focus away from personal growth and development, and it is parents' role to make sure that their kids are working on their personal skills and mental development too.

Who does not love extra play time? Everyone loves to play more, but it does not mean getting angry and throwing stuff into the walls when playtime ends or is cut short. There are many ways to deal with the anger and tantrums of your kid. The best way to help them calm themselves down is to get them busy and engaged with other activities. The following activities will help distract your kids from their aggressive behavior.

DRAWING EMOTIONS

The best way to regulate emotions is to understand them. Drawing and coloring are an integral part of kids' growth, and combining the art of drawing with emotional understanding will make it easy for kids to control their emotions. This activity will help kids understand and control their emotions while being creative and having fun.

Here is what kids should do:

- Draw pictures of different feelings and color them according to their mood, for example, kids can draw a happy face and color it pink, and an angry face and color it red. Let kids draw different emotions with the colors of their choices.

- Kids can also play a game where they can ask each other fun questions about feelings and emotions to understand others' emotions.

WRITING

Writing is an expressive way to understand emotions. Even kids who are shy and lack communication skills can express their emotions through writing.

- Ask your kids to write about their day at the end of the day.

- Ask them to be detailed while writing about how they are feeling right now, how they felt during the day, and what made them feel angry, sad, or anxious.

This activity will help them express their emotions by writing about their frustration and anger in a journal or paper which will help calm them down. If this activity is done in a group, it will increase empathy and regard for others' emotions, and it can be very helpful in making kids master their emotions.

BE A ROLE MODEL

Kids follow their parents and elders while they are still learning about life. If you want your kids to learn emotional control, help them learn by being a role model to them. When you feel sad, angry, or frustrated, share your feelings with your kids in a calm and composed manner. It will help you build trust with them, and encourage them to openly share their feelings with you, resulting in honing of their emotional regulation.

Sharing emotions will help kids in being more expressive about their emotions and in understanding that they can have different emotions. The best thing about this activity is that kids will learn to process different emotions in a safe and friendly environment.

PHYSICAL ACTIVITIES

Exercises and yoga are some of the best forms of physical activities for kids who lack calming skills and emotional regulation. Exercise increases the flow of oxygen to different organs of the body and improves moods, energy, and confidence level, which in turn reduce any negative emotions.

MINDFUL ACTIVITIES

You can understand your kid's emotions by creating a scenario where they act out different responses to particular situations. Complete the following activity by asking your kid to write a response to a situation in two different ways, a healthy and an unhealthy one.

Do the following exercise by having your child write two responses, one healthy and one unhealthy, to a given circumstance.

IMAGINE THIS FROM THE PERSPECTIVE OF:	IMAGINE THIS FROM THE PERSPECTIVE OF:
Personal views	Personal views
Emotions	Emotions
Behavior	Behavior

2.3 IMPORTANCE OF OUTDOOR ACTIVITIES TO MASTER EMOTIONS

Outdoor play is especially useful in times of stress, anxiety, and adversity because it gives kids a sense of autonomy and control, helps them understand concepts they find difficult to grasp, and supports their emotional coping and resilience.

Playing outdoors is also proven to reduce stress hormone levels in the brain, which helps to ease anxiety and stress. A recent research suggests that even five to ten minutes of vigorous activity in the outdoor space can have a profound effect on young people's emotional and psychological well-being. Here are some outdoor activities that you can perform with your kids.

SCAVENGER HUNT

Arrange a scavenger hunt for kids in the backyard or a nearby playground.

Divide the players into two teams.

After each round, change the leader of the team and help your kid understand that the performance of the team varies when the leader is calm and has control over their emotions to when their emotions are out of control.

A practical example of calmness using sports is the best way to teach kids the importance of calming skills.

You can use the scavenger hunt activities below and arrange something similar by yourself too.

LOOK FOR ANYTHING THAT:

1. Is Pink
2. Has 6 sides
3. Is much longer than a scale
4. Is shorter than a toothpick

LOOK FOR ANYTHING THAT:

1. Has alphabets on it
2. Has the letter C on it
3. Is larger than you
4. Has a smooth texture

WALKING

Walking has proven to be an effective method of regulating strong emotions. Take your kids outside for a walk and ask them to walk barefoot on the grass to benefit from the sensory touch of grass on their feet that can calm their emotions down.

Kids can also run or jog daily for better physical health while improving their emotional control and regulation.

CLOUD WATCHING

Watching natural sceneries is among some of the best calming tools for people of any age, especially for kids. Take your kids outdoors to watch clouds and trees when they are overwhelmed by emotions, and help them breathe fresh air out in the open. This activity will help kids calm their nerves and learn to control their emotions in a better way.

BIRDS AND TREES

Similar to watching and following clouds, kids can find peace in watching birds and trees. Encourage the habit of bird watching and make your kid write the names of every bird they see so they can find and document various facts about different bird species. This can be a great activity for kids as they usually find peace and calmness by closely watching birds while building their general knowledge.

ART AND DRAWING

Take your kids to the side of a lake and ask them to replicate the scene they love the most. If you cannot find time to plan a trip, you can take them to your backyard or to the nearest park and ask them to draw.

This activity will bring out creativity in kids while helping them to calm their nerves and emotions. Breathing outdoors in the fresh air will also help them stay active, energetic, and physically fit.

I-SPY

This is a fun and interactive game that gives kids a chance to use their imagination and creativity while playing. It can also improve their communication skills while teaching them to be calm and composed.

How to play?

This is a simple game played in a group outside where each player, on their turn choose an object and then shouts, "I spy something..." to describe a characteristic of the object they have picked like its color, texture, etc. Every other player has to find what the target object is by taking instructions from the lead player.

ROCKS COLLECTION

Rock collecting is one of the best hobbies one can have to spend some good time outside. It teaches kids to look and care for the smallest of details because of the similarities in shapes, colors, and sizes of numerous rocks. Rock collection gives kids a chance to learn patience, which ultimately helps them in improving their calming skills.

THE STORY OF A GRUMPY MONKEY

Parents should read this story to their kids to help them understand the message in this story and ask them to perform the activity at the end.

Once upon a time, in a dense jungle, there lived a grumpy monkey named George. George was a very cranky monkey who never seemed to be happy. He would grumble and complain about everything, from the weather to the other animals in the jungle.

One day, George woke up in a very bad mood. He grumbled as he climbed down from his tree and scowled at the other animals as they greeted him. George was so angry that he started throwing sticks and stones at the other animals. They all scattered, afraid of George's temper.

George did not care that he was scaring the other animals away. He just kept on grumbling and complaining. George's bad mood continued throughout the day, and he did not enjoy anything he usually did. He even snapped at his friend, the wise old owl, when she tried to offer him some advice.

As the sun started to set, George was still feeling angry and frustrated. He climbed up to his tree and sat their alone. Suddenly, he heard a soft rustling in the bushes below. George looked down and saw a small rabbit who looked lost and scared.

George had never seen this rabbit before, and he was surprised by how frightened it looked. Instead of throwing things at the rabbit, George decided to help the rabbit. He climbed down from his tree and approached the little creature.

George asked the rabbit what was wrong. The rabbit explained that it was lost and could not find its way back home. George realized he could use his knowledge of the jungle to help the rabbit. So, he showed the rabbit the way home, and the little creature hopped away happily.

George felt a warm feeling in his heart as he watched the rabbit run towards its home, and realized that helping the rabbit had made him happy, something he had not felt in a long time. George realized that he had been so focused on his problems and frustrations that he had forgotten about the joy that comes from helping others.

From that day on, George promised himself to be calm and friendly. He learned that being grumpy and frustrated all the time did not solve anything, but being empathic made him feel much better. George became a much happier monkey, and he lived the rest of his days in the jungle, surrounded by his friends and filled with joy.

ACTIVITY

What did you learn from this story of a grumpy monkey? Write your answer and explain why you should never be grumpy.

CHAPTER 3: MASTERING FRUSTRATION: HELP YOUR KIDS NOT TO BECOME A GRUMPY MONKEY

Grumpy kids are always a challenge for parents, which is why it's necessary to teach kids about controlling their emotions. Kids who are frustrated and angry most of the time get overwhelmed by their emotions and lose their focus and concentration. With the help of the activities in this chapter, parents can help their kids gain more focus and control their emotions. However, before solving the problems, parents will have to understand why kids become grumpy and how by learning calming skills, they can excel academically and increase their focus. Let's teach kids some skills to stay calm!

3.1 FRUSTRATION AND LOSS OF FOCUS

A child's capacity to concentrate and learn can be significantly impacted by frustration. When a child becomes frustrated, their brain releases stress hormones, impacting their ability to concentrate and learn.

LOSS OF FOCUS

Frustration can make children more easily distracted, as their mind becomes preoccupied with their emotions rather than the task at hand. This can make it difficult for them to focus on what they are learning.

DECREASED MOTIVATION

When children become frustrated, they may lose motivation to continue trying. They may feel like they are not capable of completing the task or that their efforts are not paying off. This can lead to a decrease in their interest and engagement in activities.

NEGATIVE SELF-TALK

Frustration can trigger negative self-talk, undermining a child's confidence and focus. Kids may start to believe that they are not smart enough, which may result in increased levels of stress, anxiety, or even self-harm.

PHYSICAL TENSION

Frustration can cause physical tension in the body, making it harder for kids to concentrate and focus.

3.2 WHAT MAKES YOUR KID FRUSTRATED?

Kids can get frustrated for numerous reasons and it depends upon many factors, including age, environment, and genes:

LACK OF CONTROL

Kids may become frustrated if they feel they have no control over a situation or decision. This can be easily fixed by giving them some control over different situations and involving them in the decision-making process. Parents can take help from their kids on routine tasks such as designing weekly and monthly budgets and buying groceries to help them feel that they are in control.

EXPECTATIONS

Expecting children to perform tasks or behave in ways that are beyond their capabilities can make them frustrated. The best way to deal with this situation is to avoid unrealistic expectations from kids.

BOREDOM

Children who are not stimulated or engaged may become frustrated and restless. Parents can fix this by keeping kids engaged with various indoor and outdoor activities included in the book to get rid of boredom and frustration.

SOCIAL ANXIETY

Children who struggle with social interactions may become frustrated when they are unable to connect with others. It is better to get them into therapy and teach them communication skills to deal with awkward social situations.

STRUGGLING WITH STUDY

Children who have difficulty with schoolwork may become frustrated when they are unable to keep up with their peers. Give more time to your kid if they are a slow learner and need more time to process and learn new things.

ACTIVITY

Make your kid complete this activity to understand the reasons for their frustration. Understanding a problem is the first step toward its solution, which is why this activity is important.

WRITE FIVE REASONS FOR YOUR FRUSTRATION.

3.3 HELP YOUR KIDS STAY CALM

By now, you would have told your kids the story of the grumpy monkey, and I am sure they want to be like the calm, empathetic, and happy monkey from the end of the story. Let's teach them how to stay calm and what to do when they are feeling angry or frustrated.

INDOOR CALMING ACTIVITIES

READING

Reading a book can be a calming activity for kids. Choose books that are soothing or have a calming effect.

MINDFUL BREATHING

Help your kid take deep breaths through the nose and out through the mouth. Counting while breathing can be a helpful way to keep track of the breaths.

DRAWING AND COLORING

Drawing or coloring can be a calming activity that allows kids to express themselves creatively.

BUBBLE BATH

A bath can be a calming and relaxing activity for kids. Adding some bubbles or essential oils can enhance the experience.

PUZZLES AND BOARD GAMES

Doing a puzzle can be a calming activity that requires focus and concentration. Playing a quiet game such as chess or checkers can be a soothing activity for kids.

Help your child perform a few of the tasks below whenever they feel frustrated and need to calm themselves. Take a printout of these activities and keep a copy in your bag or paste it into your living room.

SENSORY TOYS

Playing with sensory toys such as play dough or kinetic sand can be a calming activity for kids. These can also help with concentration and focus.

CIRCLE THE TOYS THAT MIGHT HELP YOU TO CALM DOWN WHEN YOU ARE FEELING NERVOUS OR ANXIOUS.

OUTDOOR ACTIVITIES

ROCK PAINTING

Collect rocks and paint them with colors. Leave them outside for others to find or use as decoration in your garden.

GARDENING

Gardening can be a calming and rewarding activity for kids. Let your kids look after a small garden bed and plant flowers in it.

BLOW THE WORRIES AWAY

Blowing bubbles can be a calming activity for children, especially when kids blow bubbles to blow their worries away. Try making a bubble solution and see who can blow the biggest bubble.

BALLOON VOLLEYBALL

Blow up a balloon and play a game of volleyball, using your hands or a makeshift net.

LEAF RUBBINGS

Collect leaves of different shapes and sizes and use crayons to make rubbings.

HIKING

Take a hike on a nearby trail, and explore the sights and sounds of the forest.

3.4 WHY NOT HELP KIDS TO BE COOL LIKE A CUCUMBER?

There are numerous ways you can teach kids to be calm and cool, like a cucumber. Here are some more activities to help you teach your kid calming skills and how to get rid of their frustration and master emotions.

ART PROJECTS

Art is a great way for kids to express themselves and let their creativity flow. Encourage them to explore different mediums, such as painting, drawing, or sculpting.

COOKING AND BAKING

Cooking or baking can be a fun and calming activity for kids. Encourage them to help out in the kitchen and to try out new recipes.

GAMES

Playing games with friends or family can be a fun and relaxing way to spend time. Encourage kids to play board games, card games, or video games.

PETS

Spending time with pets can be very calming and soothing for kids. Encourage them to spend time with pets, either by playing with them or taking care of them.

PRACTICE GRATITUDE

Teach children to express appreciation and gratitude by concentrating on the things they have to be thankful for, which may make them feel happier and more content.

BREATHING EXERCISES

Kids should practice mindful breathing, which involves paying attention to the breathing and can help them stay calm and focused.

DIFFERENT BREATHING TECHNIQUES

Here are some fun and mindful breathing exercises for kids:

BELLY BREATHING

Help your kids lie down on their backs with their hands on their bellies. Instruct them to take a few deep breaths with their nose, feeling their belly expand, and then a few slow breaths through their mouth, feeling their belly contract.

EQUAL BREATHING

Have your kids count to four as they breathe in through their nose, and then four as they breathe out through their mouth.

STRAW BREATHING

Give your child a straw and ask them to take slow breaths in and out through the straw.

FLOWER BREATHING

Ask your kids to imagine smelling a flower as they breathe in through their noses and then blowing out a candle as they breathe out through their mouths.

TRIANGLE BREATHING

Teach your children to breathe properly by having them take in four deep breaths, hold their breath for the next four counts and then release four quick, shallow breaths.

LION'S BREATH

Make your kids breathe like a lion by asking them to breathe deeply through their noses and then stick their tongues out and exhale loudly like a lion's roar.

BUNNY BREATHING

Ask your kids to take quick, short breaths through their noses like a bunny sniffing a carrot.

HUMMING BEE BREATH

Go outside and ask your kids to breathe in deeply through their noses and then exhale with a humming sound like a bee.

SNAKE BREATHING

Have your kids breathe in deeply through their noses and then hiss like a snake as they exhale slowly through their mouths.

OCEAN BREATHING

In this breathing technique, ask your kids to imagine that they are sitting on a beach, and as they breathe in deeply through their noses, they imagine the sound of the waves crashing. As they exhale slowly through their mouth, they imagine the waves rolling back out to sea.

SOUP BREATHING

1. Now, picture yourself with a steaming cup of soup in your hands.
2. Sniff the soup by taking deep, slow breaths through your nose.
3. Exhale slowly through your lips to reduce the temperature of the soup.
4. Repeated as often as necessary.

RAINBOW BREATHING

COLORFUL EXHALATION

1. Visualize a rainbow arcing in front of you.

2. While taking a deep breath in through your nose, trace the rainbow with your finger from left to right.

3. While gently exhaling through your lips, draw the rainbow from right to left.

4. Repeat 4 times or until the desired effect is achieved.

DEEP BREATHING

CALMING BREATHING EXERCISE

The target is the white dot, so put your finger there. Follow the arrow and relax for a moment. Wait until the arrow stops.

Follow the direction of the following arrow and exhale. Keep going until you've completed numerous complete circles around the image.

50

STAR BREATHING

Calming breathing exercise: To perform the exercise, pick any "Breathe in" side and proceed to hold your breath till the point before breathing out.

Don't stop until you've gone all the way around the star.

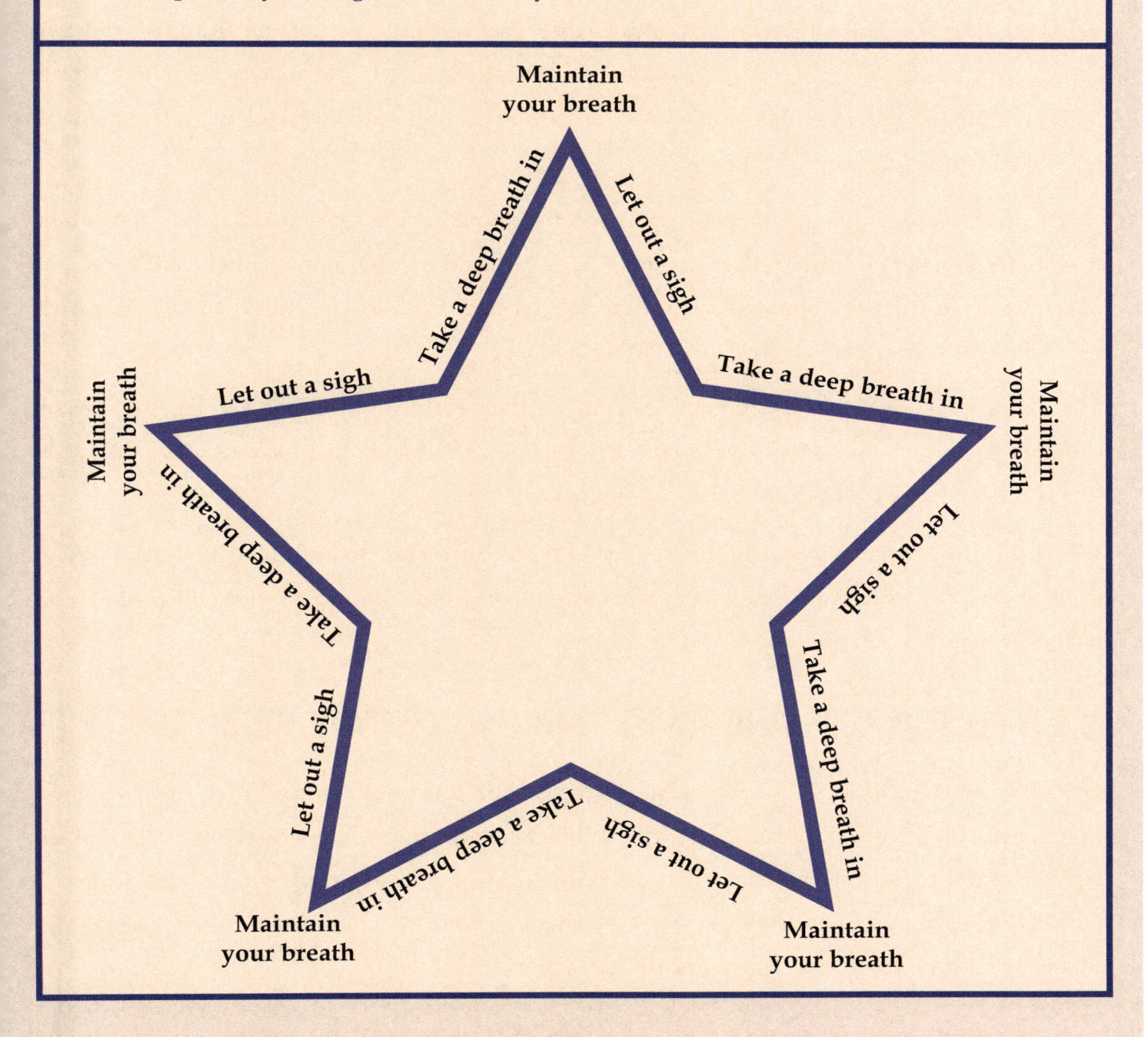

- Maintain your breath
- Take a deep breath in
- Let out a sigh
- Maintain your breath
- Take a deep breath in
- Let out a sigh
- Maintain your breath
- Take a deep breath in
- Let out a sigh
- Maintain your breath
- Take a deep breath in
- Let out a sigh
- Maintain your breath

CHAPTER 4: HELP YOUR KID FIND CALMNESS THROUGH CBT

Before starting Cognitive Behavioral Therapy (CBT) for their kids, parents must understand that CBT is not a miracle that will help their kids cope with stress, anger, and anxiety overnight. This is a gradual process done through a series of exercises and activities to help kids who struggle with emotional regulation.

CBT focuses on identifying and challenging negative thought patterns and behaviors, and can be used to treat anxiety disorders, depression, OCD, PTSD, and ADHD, among other conditions. The effectiveness of CBT is not limited to these conditions, and it can also be effective in teaching kids self-control, emotional regulation, and calming skills.

This chapter first discusses the importance and effectiveness of CBT for kids and then focuses on different techniques and activities used in CBT to help kids through the problems they face due to low self-esteem, lower self-control, and no emotional control.

CBT is a highly effective treatment for a range of problems related to mental health in children. It can help children overcome negative thought patterns and behaviors and develop coping skills and resilience that they can use throughout their lives.

4.1 EFFECTIVENESS AND IMPORTANCE OF CBT FOR KIDS

One of the key benefits of CBT is that it is a relatively short-term treatment. CBT is a relatively brief treatment, which is one of its most significant advantages. Most children who receive CBT will see significant improvement in their symptoms within a few months of starting treatment. This can particularly be important for children who are struggling with school or other activities, as it allows them to get back to their normal routine more quickly.

Children can benefit from CBT in other ways as well, including the development of key life skills that can serve them for the rest of their lives. CBT can help children, for example, learn how to solve problems, talk to others effectively, and feel better about themselves. These abilities may be useful in many aspects of life, including education, job, and interpersonal relations. By providing children with effective treatment for their mental health challenges, CBT can help them feel more confident and empowered. It can also help raise awareness about the importance of mental health and encourage them to seek help when needed. The most significant advantage of using CBT treatment over other treatment is that it tends to the needs of the patient in a particularly designed way which is specific to the patient. It focuses on the way an individual behaves and thinks and then identifies strategies to cope with and eliminate any negative behaviors.

EFFECTIVENESS OF CBT

HELPING WITH EATING DISORDERS

More than 50% of kids aged 9-12 have some form of eating disorder which reduce to 13% by the time they turn 20. These eating disorders are one of the main causes of weight loss, anxiety, and lower self-esteem in kids and teens, and CBT can help kids with addressing these challenges along with reducing the chances of mood swings and outbursts, resulting in the calmness of emotions.

DEFIANCE DISORDER

ODD, commonly called Oppositional Defiant Disorder, is common in kids and young teens. Kids with ODD show restrictive and hostile behavior toward all authority figures resulting in negative and hostile behavior. CBT can treat ODD and support the development of calming skills in kids. Through CBT treatment, kids learn to control their defiance and be less hostile, resulting in mastering of their emotional control, which reduces their frustration and anger.

SELF-HARM, SELF-LOVE, AND SELF-ESTEEM

Kids suffering from anxiety are more susceptible to have low self-confidence and low self-love, resulting in self-harm, with banging of heads against the walls as the initial and most common form, and even suicide attempts at early ages. CBT can help kids get the necessary help they need to boost their self-esteem, increase their self-love, and prevent them from self-harm.

BULLYING

Among school-going kids, bullying is the most common negative phenomenon. Kids affected by bullying at school are most likely to have anxiety and emotional imbalance. Several researchers have proved that CBT is effective against the impacts of bullying and can help kids gain emotional balance and stay calm in bad situations.

SUBSTANCE USE

12 is a critical age where some kids may start substance use due to psychological pressure and social challenges. If kids are experiencing continuous discomfort, anger, and anxiety, CBT can help keep kids safe from substance use as confirmed by many researchers.

IMPORTANCE OF CBT

SELF-CONTROL

CBT can increase kids' self-control and help them enhance their problem-solving and social skills. Improvement in self-control increases the chance of developing calming skills, emotional balance, and getting rid of frustration.

ANXIETY AND STRESS

Kids from ages 9-12 can benefit greatly from CBT treatments to reduce their anxiety, stress, and anger issues.

PTSD AND CHILDHOOD TRAUMAS

CBT focused on trauma-based treatments can help kids with PTSD and childhood traumas and can be effective in reducing stress related to abuse, shame, and harm.

SOCIAL SKILLS

CBT helps kids to learn basic social skills and improve interpersonal skills significantly.

COMMUNICATION SKILLS

CBT helps kids with communication issues to express themselves freely, improving their emotional expression to the extent that they can express themselves comfortably and learn to control their emotions.

SLEEP DISORDERS

CBT helps treat sleep disorders that some kids may experience due to stress, anxiety, and emotional imbalance.

4.2 HELPING KIDS COPE WITH STRESS, ANXIETY, AND ANGER THROUGH CBT

This section will explain how to perform various CBT exercises and activities to help kids cope with stress, anxiety, and anger.

CBT FOR ANXIETY

CBT is an effective technique against generalized and social anxiety in kids. The main aim of this technique is to develop skills that will help in better emotional responses. Negative thoughts lead to negative feelings and result in negative responses, and CBT will help in fighting these negative thoughts and alter kids' thinking through a 3-staged process:

IDENTIFICATION

The first step in this process is the identification of a negative thought. For example, a kid might think that if they cannot answer the questions in the classroom, they must be a loser. Through CBT techniques and therapy sessions, the origin of this negative thought will be uncovered. Kids can share all the negative thoughts one by one and solve them separately.

CHALLENGE

The next step in this process is to challenge the negative thought and analyze its reality. This step identifies the logical reason behind the negative thought. For example, "you feel like a loser for not being able to answer a question because someone called you a loser once for the same reason."

The main part of this step is to challenge the reality of the negative thoughts. For example, by saying, "no one thinks you are a loser just because you could not answer the question. This thought was generated in your own mind and has nothing to do with reality. If your teacher thought you were a loser, they would not have asked you the question."

REPLACEMENT

The final step in this process is replacing the negative with an opposite, positive thought. For example, it could be by saying "you may feel like you are a loser for not being able to answer the questions, but others do not see you as a loser and think you are smart".

The repetition of this three-step process for various negative thoughts will help in coping with anxiety and help kids in controlling their emotions.

CBT FOR STRESS

CBT treatment is very effective for kids dealing with stress due to psychological or academic pressure. There are various techniques used in CBT to cope with stress, and the most commonly effective ones are:

DIAPHRAGMATIC BREATHING

This is also known as belly breathing or deep breathing. This technique involves contraction and relaxation of the diaphragm between the chest and abdomen. The contraction of the diaphragm that occurs during this process results in the expansion of the lungs, which in turn allows more air to be taken into the body. The diaphragm is relaxed during exhalation, which causes the lungs to contract and the air to exit the body.

This breathing technique is effective in several ways, including:

- Reducing stress and helping calm the body.

- Improving lung function by increasing the amount of oxygen entering the body.

- Strengthening the diaphragm that makes breathing easy and efficient.

HOW TO PERFORM DIAPHRAGMATIC BREATHING?

To practice diaphragmatic breathing, find a comfortable position and place your hand on your stomach. Inhale deeply through your nose, allowing your belly to expand and your hand to move outward. Exhale slowly through your mouth, pulling your belly button toward your spine. Repeat this process several times, taking slow, deep breaths and focusing on the sensation of your diaphragm contracting and relaxing.

PROGRESSIVE MUSCLE RELAXATION (PMR)

In this technique, different muscle groups from the body are tensed and relaxed, one at a time. It can be a helpful tool for kids to manage stress and anxiety and to improve their overall well-being.

- Help your child find a quiet and comfortable place to practice PMR. This could be a bedroom, living room, or any space where they feel safe and relaxed.

- Begin with a few deep breaths to help your child relax and focus their attention on the present moment.

- Starting with the feet, tell your child to tense their muscles in their feet area by squeezing them tightly for a few seconds, then releasing the tension and relaxing for 10-15 seconds. Move up the body, repeating this process with each muscle group, including the legs, abdomen, arms, shoulders, and face.

- As you guide your child through each muscle group, encourage them to focus on the sensation of tension and relaxation in their body. You can ask questions such as "What does it feel like when you tense your leg muscles?" or "How does it feel when you relax your face muscles?"

- After completing all the muscle groups, end the session with a few deep breaths to help your child fully relax and release any remaining tension.

It's essential to bear in mind that even though PMR can help kids deal with stress and anxiety, it shouldn't be used instead of professional mental health care if that's what they need. If your child is experiencing persistent or severe anxiety, consider seeking the guidance of a mental health professional.

MEDITATION

Meditation can be a great tool for kids to cope with stress. Here are some steps to guide kids through a basic meditation practice:

- Find a quiet and comfortable place.

- Have your child sit in a comfortable position with their legs crossed, hands resting on their knees, and eyes closed.

- Encourage your child to focus their attention on their breathing. They can count their breaths or simply focus on the sensation of air moving in and out of their body.

- As thoughts and feelings arise, encourage your child to observe them without judgment. They can imagine their thoughts and feelings as clouds passing by in the sky and then gently bring their attention back to their breathing.

- After a few minutes of focusing on the breathing and observing thoughts and feelings, end the session with a moment of gratitude. Have your child think of something they are grateful for, and spend a few moments reflecting on that feeling of gratitude.

It's important to note that meditation can be challenging for kids, especially at first. Encourage your child to practice regularly, and allow them to take breaks if they are frustrated or overwhelmed. Gradually increase the length of the sessions as their ability to focus and sit still improves.

MINDFULNESS PRACTICES

These are different practices approved by CBT specialists that can help kids to cope with anxiety and stress:

- Encourage your child to focus on their breathing, counting each inhale and exhales. This can be a helpful way to calm their mind and bring awareness to the present moment.

- Encourage your child to pay attention to the taste, smell, and texture of their food. Have them take small bites and chew slowly, focusing on the sensation of each bite.

- Take your child for a walk and encourage them to pay attention to the sensation of the ground on their feet, the movement of their body, and the sights and sounds around them.

- Guide your child through a body scan meditation and have them focus on each part of their body to bring awareness to any sensations they may be feeling.

- Have your child write down three things they are grateful for each day. This can help them develop a positive mindset and cultivate a sense of gratitude.

- Coloring is another way to help your kid to cope with stress.

HERE ARE SOME COLORING ACTIVITIES FOR KIDS:

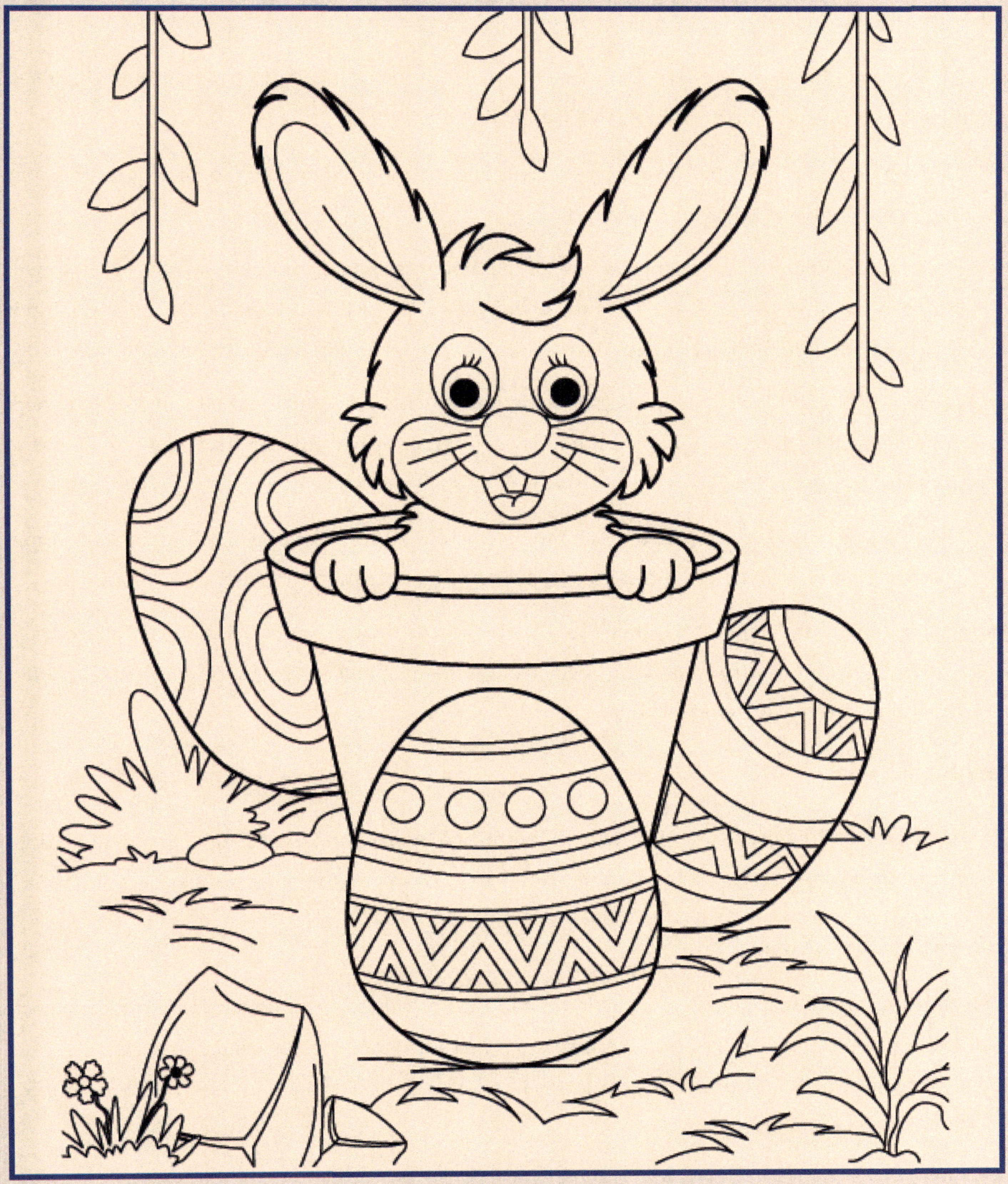

CBT FOR ANGER

CBT has proven to be an effective and efficient approach toward teaching kids calming skills and helping them cope with anger issues. This can be done by:

- Helping your child identify what triggers their anger. This could be situations, people, or events that make them feel angry or frustrated.

- Encouraging your child to become aware of the thoughts and beliefs contributing to their anger. For example, they may believe that they are always right or that things should always go their way. Sit with them and help them understand that things might not always go their way.

- Teaching your child to challenge negative thoughts and beliefs contributing to anger. Help them understand that their thoughts are not always accurate or helpful and that they can choose to think differently.

- Helping your child use relaxation techniques such as deep breathing, PMR, or visualization. These techniques can help them calm down when they feel angry or frustrated.

- Helping them understand that there are different ways to approach a problem, and encourage them to consider multiple solutions. Kids can use problem-solving skills when they encounter situations that make them feel angry.

PENT-UP ANGER

Some kids have difficulty expressing their anger through words, and they usually avoid and ignore their frustration and anger. CBT techniques can help kids cope with pent-up anger.

SELF-DIRECTED ANGER

Self-directed anger is a behavior in which a child directs their anger towards themselves, such as hitting or biting themselves, pulling their own hair, or banging their head against a wall. This behavior can be a sign of underlying emotional imbalance. CBT can be an effective treatment for self-directed anger in kids.

VOLATILE ANGER

Volatile anger in kids is characterized by sudden outbursts of intense anger that may result in physical aggression toward other people or property, which can be helped and corrected with CBT.

4.3 WANT YOUR KIDS TO HAVE MORE CONTROL OVER THEIR TEMPER THROUGH CBT?

Teaching kids how to manage their temper is an important skill that will benefit them throughout their lives. CBT can help kids manage anxiety, stress, and anger, however, parents must teach kids to control their temper through calming skills. There are several activities you can participate in with your kid to get their temper under control.

COUNTING

Tell your child to count backwards from 10 (or higher) when they are angry or upset. This can help them calm down and think more clearly before reacting.

VISUALIZATION

Encourage your child to imagine a peaceful place or situation when they feel angry or frustrated. For example, they could imagine themselves on a beach or in a forest.

EXERCISE AND PHYSICAL ACTIVITY

Engage your child in physical activity such as running, jumping, or dancing. This can help them positively release their pent-up emotions and get their temper under control.

KEEP A JOURNAL

Encourage your child to write down their thoughts and feelings when they feel angry or upset. This can help them process their emotions and gain a better understanding of what triggered their loss of temper.

Here is a list of journaling worksheets that your child can complete.

If you're feeling nervous or irritated, you may start thinking a lot of bad things. Your mood won't improve as a result of these ideas. How about you think about some good things that will help you relax?

THINGS THAT MADE ME GIGGLE TODAY:

THINGS THAT MADE ME SAD TODAY:

THINGS THAT I STARTED WORRYING ABOUT TODAY:

THE BEST FEELING IN THE DAY WAS:

I AM GRATEFUL FOR:

THINGS THAT I LOOK FORWARD TO AND THAT MAKE ME EXCITED:

Be brave enough to accept yourself with all your flaws. Be hopeful enough to know that you will overcome them one day.

Write down three things that you feel most proud about yourself in the hearts given below.

ROLE-PLAYING

Use role-playing to help your child practice managing their temper in different situations. For example, you could pretend to be a sibling who is annoying them and teach them how to respond in a calm and assertive way.

Please remember that all these activities should be completed with the kids when they are not angry or frustrated, so they can participate in them with a clear head and learn to identify when they need to control their temper.

Practice the following to keep kids' temper in control:

- Teach your child to recognize when they are getting angry and encourage them to take a break from the situation.

- Help your child understand how their words and actions affect others. Encourage them to put themselves in other people's shoes and consider their feelings before reacting.

- Encourage your child to use humor to diffuse tense situations. A well-timed joke or silly comment can help to lighten the mood.

- Praise your child when they handle their emotions well. This will reinforce positive behaviors and encourage them to continue using these techniques.

It is important to model positive behavior and use these techniques yourself, so your child can see how to handle their emotions in a healthy way.

Here are some CBT activities your kids can perform to get better at controlling their emotions.

Are You Experiencing Overwhelming Difficulty?

It's important to remember the "RAIN" four-step process to help us ease off on our self-criticism.

R	A	I	N
Recognize the present situation	Accept the experience for what it is.	Investigate Nicely.	Natural awareness that arises from detaching oneself from an experience.

Here are four steps to snap out of your difficulties and live a healthy and happy life.

S	N	A	P
Stop everything that you are doing when you feel like you are being provoked.	Notice the reactions that are going in your mind and body.	Allow yourself to accept the reality and experience it.	Prompt yourself to be gentle with yourself.

CALM DOWN DEVICES

1. Breathe in for three seconds and then breathe out for ten seconds.

2. Play some music or sing a song.

3. Put your hands in your pocket.

4. Hug your loved ones.

5. Take a deep breath and exhale into your hands.

6. Create a visual representation of how you feel.

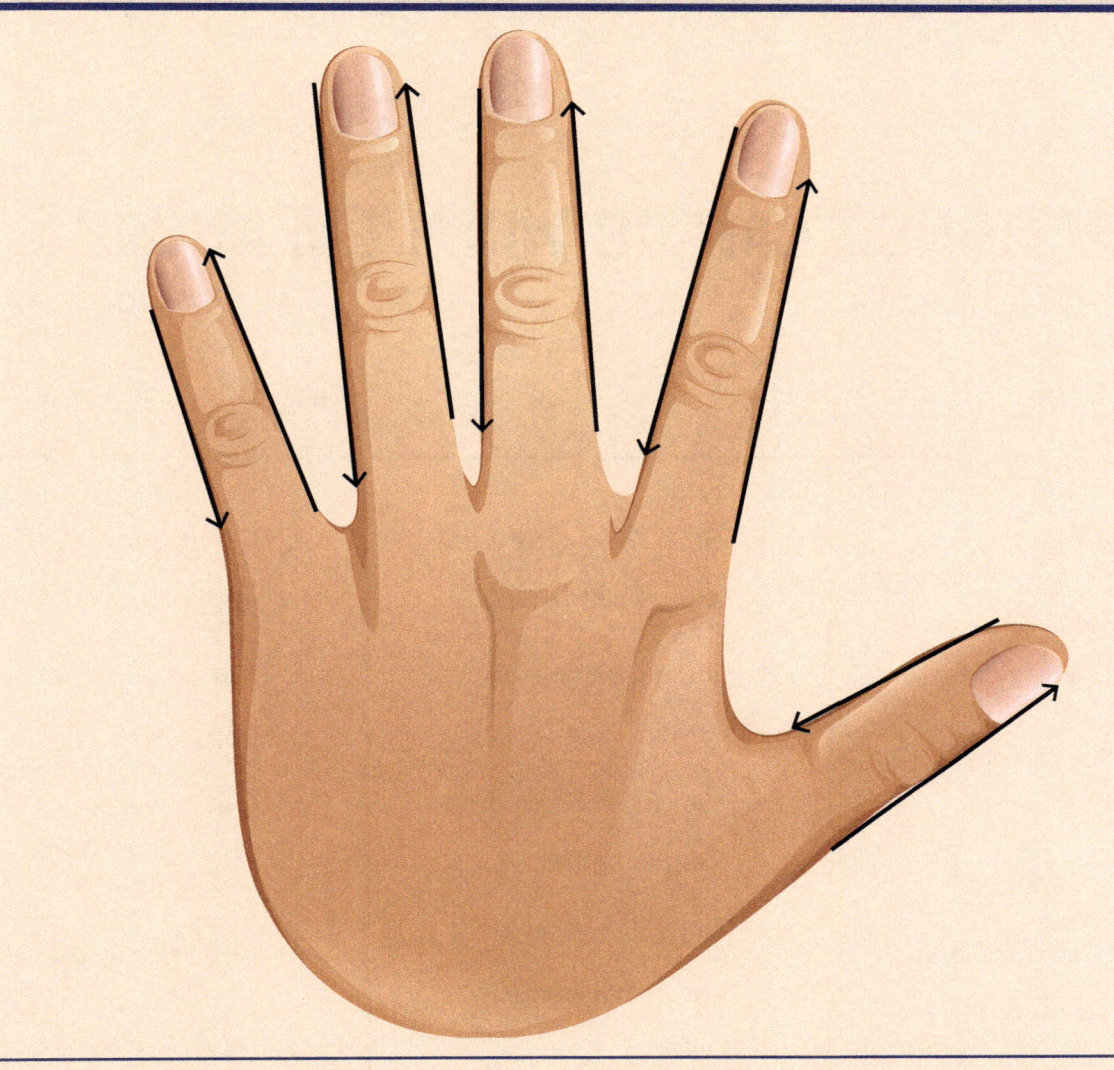

1. Leave some space between the fingers of one hand.

2. Raise your other index finger to your thumb.

3. Your thumb's base should be your starting point.

4. While you take a deep breath in through your mouth, draw the thumb's outline with your index finger.

5. When your finger reaches the tip of your thumb and you are working your way down the opposite side, exhale slowly through your nose.

6. Once you've traced one finger, repeat the process for the rest of your fingers.

ACTIONS I CAN DO WHEN I'M ANGRY

- Compress a ball
- Make a yoga position
- Pucker up some Play-Doh
- Do ten push-ups
- Get a discount on a happy lunch
- Put on a silly expression
- Create a new dance step

- Stop for a moment and count to ten
- Drink a glass of water
- Get dressed up and snap a selfie.
- Start at 100 and count backwards till 5
- Write a song
- Giggle
- Meditate

- Go outside and enjoy the weather
- Put on an act of happiness
- Get assistance
- Get some rest
- Be angry and draw it
- Play some tunes for me
- Dial a Friend
- Have a Frisbee game
- Do some planting

WHAT DID YOU LEARN?

This section is included for parents and kids to record what they have learned through this book so far and how will they respond to various situations.

FOR PARENTS

Parents need to take a paper and answer the following questions:

What did you learn about the emotions of your kid? Is your kid expressive or shy?

How often does your kid have a tantrum?

Did you make any progress with your kid with the help of this book?

Is your kid better at emotional control than before?

FOR KIDS

Kids, what did you learn from this book? Answer the following questions:

What makes you anxious, stressed, or angry?

Does anyone bully you at school? If yes, how do you respond to it?

What makes you feel relaxed and happy?

FINAL WORDS

This book is a great resource for parents, teachers, and other care takers who wish to encourage kids to learn good coping mechanisms for anxiety, stress, and other unpleasant emotions. The workbook offers a variety of practical and engaging activities designed to help children build resilience, improve emotional regulation, and teach them calming skills.

The workbook is organized into sections, each of which focuses on a distinct component of calming and self-regulation. Each section of this book teaches children how to control their anger and introduces them to several mindful breathing and calming activities. Parents can also learn these strategies to help kids deal with their anxiety and anger issues.

Each activity encourages children to think about their own experiences and emotions and to develop a deeper understanding of their thought processes and behaviors. Another strength of the book is its use of creative and interactive activities. Rather than relying solely on written exercises, this book offers a variety of engaging activities that appeal to children's different learning styles and interests. There are drawing and cut-and-paste activities, mindfulness games, and journaling prompts that allow children to express themselves in different ways and engage with the material in a meaningful manner to learn calming skills and master their emotions.

GOODBYE MESSAGE FOR KIDS!

As you come to the end of the book, I want to say big congratulations to you for taking the time to learn and practice these important skills. I hope that you found the activities helpful and that you feel more confident in managing your emotions and finding peace in difficult situations. Remember that calming skills are something that you can continue to practice and build upon throughout your life. When you feel overwhelmed or stressed, take a moment to use one of the techniques you have learned in this book, whether it's deep breathing, visualization, or positive self-talk to feel more in control and to approach challenges with a sense of calm and clarity. I am so proud of your hard work, and I wish you all the best as you continue to grow and learn. Remember to always be kind to yourself and to reach out for support when you need it.

THANK YOU

Printed in Great Britain
by Amazon